Jon
Buys a Present

Story by Annette Smith
Illustrations by Xiangyi Mo
and Jingwen Wang

Mom, Dad, and Jonathan
were shopping at the market.

"I'll get some oranges
for Grandad," said Mom.
"He isn't feeling very well.
He has had a bad cold."

2

"I could buy him something
to cheer him up," said Jonathan.
"I have got my money here
with me."

When Mom had bought the oranges
and some vegetables,
they had a look around
the other stalls.

"Taffy apples!" said Jonathan.
"Grandad loves taffy apples.
I'll get one for him!"

Jonathan bought
a big taffy apple.

"Mm-mm," he said.
"It smells good.
I'll just give it a little lick."

Jonathan gave the taffy apple
a lick, and then he took
a bite out of it.

"I can't give it to Grandad now,"
he said.
"**I'll** have to eat it."

Mom, Dad, and Jonathan went
over to the toy stall.

"I'll get Grandad some marbles,"
said Jonathan.

"Yes," said Dad,
"Grandad is always telling us
how good he was at playing marbles."

Jonathan bought a bag of marbles.
He held them up and looked at them.
They were shiny.

"I would like to keep these marbles,"
he said.
"I could take them to school."

Jonathan put the marbles
in his pocket.
"I've still got some money left,"
he said to Dad.
They went on to the next stall.

"A puppet!" said Jonathan. "Yes, that's it!
Grandad would have lots of fun
with a puppet because he likes
playing tricks.
Here's a crocodile puppet!"

Jonathan looked at the crocodile puppet.
Then he looked at his money.
"Oh, no!" he said. "I can't buy
a puppet for Grandad, after all."

12

Mom smiled.
"You and Dad can keep looking
for something, Jonathan," she said.
"I'm going to buy some new plants
for the garden."

Dad and Jonathan
went around the corner
to the next stall.
When they came back,
they were laughing.

Jonathan had something
hidden behind his back.

"Well?" said Mom.
"What did you get
for Grandad?"

"What does Grandad like doing best of all?" said Dad.

"Well, he does like playing tricks on us," said Mom.

"Look!" said Jonathan.
"This will cheer him up."

"He will love it," laughed Mom.